Praise for
Oracle

"These are poems of feeling, memory, and calamity, of a life lived near the edge and an edge that nevertheless always resolves itself into a haunting ethical music. This is a wonderful collection of poems. It makes a powerful claim on the reader at every turn, on every page."
—Eavan Boland

"When action arrives in a Cate Marvin poem, it's like she's a superhero aiming incisive critiques. However, what is to be trusted here is her ear and her wry humor. No one will beg to disagree: increasingly, Cate Marvin is a force whose beseeching rhythms make her one of the most gifted poets of her generation."
—Major Jackson

"E. M. Cioran claimed that 'salvation is the death of song.' Three books in, and Cate Marvin shows no signs of having been saved. Film noir troubadour, Staten Island flâneur, metaphysical deer-stalker: this the poet of pursuant dread, of the ghost-infested Thou, and of the despairing American endlessness of self. Dark? Yes. But the balm, in *Oracle*, is the power of the Marvin-speaker's sense of humor—'I once had a quasi- / Victorian way about me'—which is at its most politic and disarming the closer it gets to the shadow."
—Josh Bell

"*Oracle* explores the devastating experiences of womanhood—hurricane season, dead girl season, break-up season—the stations she weathers as she rises from the ruin with her wits intact. Electric and triumphant, *Oracle* delivers Marvin's trademark bravado in poems about the darkly human journey."
—Rigoberto González

ORACLE

ORACLE

POEMS

CATE MARVIN

W. W. Norton & Company
Independent Publishers Since 1923
NEW YORK • LONDON

For information about permission to reproduce selections from this book,
write to Permissions, W. W. Norton & Company, Inc.,
500 Fifth Avenue, New York, NY 10110

For information about special discounts for bulk purchases, please contact
W. W. Norton Special Sales at specialsales@wwnorton.com or
800-233-4830

Manufacturing by RR Donnelley
Book design by Brooke Koven
Production managers: Devon Zahn and Ruth Toda

Library of Congress Cataloging-in-Publication Data

Marvin, Cate, 1969–
[Poems. Selections]
Oracle : poems / Cate Marvin. — First edition.
pages ; cm
ISBN 978-0-393-07798-8 (hardcover)
I. Title.
PS3563.A74294A6 2015
811'.54—dc23

2014045437

ISBN 978-0-393-35313-6 pbk.

W. W. Norton & Company, Inc.
500 Fifth Avenue, New York, N.Y. 10110
www.wwnorton.com

W. W. Norton & Company Ltd.
Castle House, 75/76 Wells Street, London W1T 3QT

1 2 3 4 5 6 7 8 9 0

I am coming back
for my wings
——FEDERICO GARCÍA LORCA

CONTENTS

ACKNOWLEDGMENTS

MANY THANKS to the editors who gave my poems a home:

Academy of American Poets website "Poem-A-Day" feature: "Why I
    Am Afraid of Turning the Page"; "Oracle"; "Plastic Cookie"
The Awl: "High School as a Dead Girl"; "High School: Indus-
    trial Arts"
The Boston Review: "Poetry Machines"
The Chronicle of Higher Education: "Let the Day Perish"
Cura: "Baffin Island"
The Harvard Review: "My First Husband Was My Last"
New England Review: "The Apparition"
The Normal School: "Dogsbody"
The Paris-American: "Poem for an Awful Girl"
Poetry: "Dead Girl Gang Bang"
The Rumpus: "After Aftermath"
Six Rings / Huffington Post: "I'll Be Back"
Sugar House Review: "Dead Fleas in a Dish Read as Tea Leaves
    in a Cup"
Tin House: "On the Ineptitude of Certain Hurricanes";
    "Thoughts on Wisteria"; "Slaughter and Wisteria"; "Chilly
    Voice in the Tropics"
Underwater New York: "Dread Beach"
Virginia Quarterly Review: "Some Day My Prince Will Come"
Volt: "A Thousand Degrees"; "High School as Remembered
    by the Dying Dog"

Washington Square: "The Hamptons"
Willow Springs: "An Etiquette for Eyes"

I am very much indebted to the generosity of the kind folks at the James Merrill House, the Corporation of Yaddo, the Professional Staff Congress of the City University of New York, the MacDowell Colony, the Texas Institute of the Arts, the New York Foundation for the Arts, and the Mrs. Giles Whiting Foundation.

I wish also to thank my editor, Jill Bialosky, as well as my agent, Betsy Lerner, who so graciously, and significantly, supported my work just at the time I found myself intellectually and psychically adrift. I'm continually cheered by the wherewithal of my dearest literary pals: Erin Belieu, Michael Dumanis, and Laurie Foos. I am more than fortunate to have parents, Charlie and Mary Jo Marvin, who never once questioned my literary inclinations. Thanks also my oldest pal, Jim Moody Wyss, and to Matthew Yeager, who never fails to get where my poetry's at. Finally, I remain grateful for the conversations that sustain me: specifically those provided by my students at the College of Staten Island, Lesley University's and Columbia University's respective MFA programs, and most especially those conducted by everyone involved with VIDA: Women and Literary Arts, past and present.

This book is dedicated to two very stubborn people:

my daughter Lucia Drew Marvin,
who is "new to the Earth."
my colleague Mary M. Reda,
who has so regrettably left us.

ORACLE

ON THE INEPTITUDE OF
CERTAIN HURRICANES

As the leering boss poised by a photocopier
might prevent a secretary from completing
a simple task, she will approach the machine,
dread-filled, ocean's stomach of inevitability—
for certainly will he lean to her shell-small

ear (pinched with a plain pearl) to impart
his jism, words jetting deep up from within
his throat: the grocery stores are ransacked.
Generators battled for. Gallons of water lugged
beneath arms to car trunks. As if we might die.

Only past midnight rain begins its sluicing
through tree branches, lashes streets' tarry
lengths, runnels its hasty murks down drains.
Wait for it to *hit*. One waits, does not sleep.
As if it's better to be struck while conscious.

Which brings us to the question of why it is
only tonight that we stay awake, lie in wait
for its punch. Brings us to the question of how
is it that we, as a highly developed species, are
even capable of sleep, since strikes lie always

in wait, even when hurricane is not a season,
this weather that cannot but be our own, is all
that of which we are ourselves capable. Stand
in cashier lines and your jawline dies to break
at the impact of an anonymous fist. Because you

talk too much. Because of your lips. Have you
not been told, in no uncertain terms, you'll die
before your time, by an individual who in no
uncertain terms wants you to die? So lie dead
to this wind, unnoose yourself from weather,

because oblivion becomes us. Waking, I clear
glasses from tables, empty ashtrays, go out for
a drive. See whole red clouds of tree heads sunk
onto sidewalks, sirens stream scarlet embers
along the surfaces of knee-deep puddles. Every

single block's been hit, minus mine. Minus me,
I can't complain. Minus me means a vacation from
me. Yet, will my lovers be concerned by my absence?
This problem is quickly solved since I have none.
Go ahead, yank my insides out. Name your pleasure.

HIGH SCHOOL AS A DEAD GIRL

High School was us and we. We learned our grammar there.
Became devised by bells sawing halls sharp as number two
pencils: we grew thin, grew dark as men in its hallways, we
grew up on men, our breasts their beards, their beards our
breasts, while we cracked open beer cans in the Girls' Room,
swug down foam minutes before walking into Homeroom.
I was known to be dumb, detentioned, a kill myself kind of
girl, but it was you who shot herself in the head. What kind
of girl shoots herself in the head? You wanted a quality kill?
Take some sleeping pills, spare your mother the blood-grief.
You always took the hit for me. Turned around in your seat.
Did you hear what they said? *Yes, some of us are intending
to go to college.* Loser grief. Then the tarry hot of the parking
lot rose up, black, promising me any boy's face bent to crack
against my face that was becoming a face: when we wanted
what we all wanted. To be *pretty*. Which then meant *famous*.

SOME DAY MY PRINCE WILL COME

I.

Angel, I'm drilling an edge of the island for oil,
fed your smashed piñata Tylenol, left it buckled
in the passenger seat. At the snap of my fingers,
your eyes will open, but you will recall nothing.

Angel, you turned your key, but your own lock
no longer fit it. She ate the mouse *and* the cat,
then ate the house! She is lowering your roof's
heated dome over her head, waiting for her curl

to set in a salon she's fashioned from your hard-
worked bones. You passed out from the fumes.
Now I'm thigh-deep and slick, no, sick in the pit
of her religion. She traded your eyes in for the last

Payday (stale) the vending machine had to offer.
She thinks she's trading up prayers, she thinks
them exchangeable as wishes. She forgot deep
slots are grave plots, Angel, as are our kisses.

II.

It seems. We must. The ferry ruts the dock.
Somewhere, someone is changing the locks.
I feel you piloting the veins of the island.
I feel feral cats stir up a clutter of attics.

If they refuse to look you in the eye, you
know they are the kind of wild that wants
nothing to do with wilderness. Snow Angel,
they appear only to snap their sooty backs

beneath an engine's heat, greased assembly
of pale flowers narrowing against a gauze
of zeros. We, too, begin kitten-deep inside
the pocket of a mother; her electrifying fur

still moves our herd toward the boat's prow,
because we are always wishing to land, greet.
I am punching your molecular code into my
forever panel. I speak the language of locks.

I'LL BE BACK

Walking very quickly makes it quite impossible
to note the lousy perfection of stars. It's why I walk
as if everything from me might be snatched should

I slow down, as if even the stars might be whisked
out from the fumes of sky, as thunder claps, cracks
my own house in half, an egg chipped at the edge

of a bowl, so that when I spill out all saffron, slide
to the corner bodega to buy a forty, no one but me
notices me, for I am crawling beneath the window

frames. I am one with the weeds and their death-
hair, an anonymous splendor, my lines zigzagging
artery all over the crushed glass, the littered potato

chip bags that fill with air to blow their small metallic
balloons toward the water that meets the end of this
street: for water socked with salt is where I'm headed

nowadays, drawing up my will as carriages once drew
up to the entrances of ballrooms, to spill gentlefolk out
in gaudy dresses, smart suits, their fans aflutter before

every face: all the faces I am willing away, except for
my ghost, his face, he who barely remembers to visit
my bedchamber since years have trimmed my hair's

length, its black sheet, split ends. I once had a quasi-
Victorian way about me, sat within my room, my quill
poised, watching the sad families stalk the sidewalk

before my window in the mercury warm pool gifted
to me by my mirror. A line does not always end having
arrived at a point. Live lowly, pull the blinds shut, drink

yourself dumb so as not to worry how you once let your
own self break into your own house through a back room
window when you accidentally shut yourself out without

keys or cash. If you can't avoid being invaded, why not
extend an invitation to your destroyer? I don't drink tea,
but I can brew it. I feed only on pomegranate. I'm that

big a fan of the underworld. It's why I'm so whittled, it's
why I don't bother with blush. I should brush my cheeks
with rose-tinted gunpowder? As if that'd make me look

more alive. I might have made a good mortician. I know
how to put a body back in its place. Crack my house open
again, I'll call my lawyer. It's called an order.

Of restraint.

THOUGHTS ON WISTERIA

You were my Maud Gonne. When black ink won.
Ran down my page like a throat slashed: attack.
Your were my bassinet. When the bough swung
down came our rock-a-bye, baby, and all those
blue-reds swum their orb-lights against fences
as cop's cars pulled their immediacy alongside
my house when you were the fence the drunk
driver smashed into in that ice-age, knocked at
an angle that cracked the frozen plastic of PVC
fencing jaggedly, still in half, it was your winter.

Once, you were nearly mine, bar lights dimmed,
but the mode of attack I always relied on dumb.
Another drink, this time a mojito. You sniffed its
sugars, downed it, then turned to grind the hip
of the girl the room liked least. I'm still shoveling
snow. I stubbed my toe. I fell down some stairs.
One might have thought I was no one. No matter
the nightgown. I was never meant to be your girl.
The snow plows are out. They are coming for me.
And how my envy grows like a tree. Summer me!

The wisteria begins as a vine, becomes a tree,
though needs more years than our species has
for it to give us notice of its blossoms, allow our
noses to ride its fine fragrance as delinquent bees

do now on hovering my neighbor's heavily piling
of growth, a vine that centuries into a tree. It is
terrible sweet. Who decides that which is flower,
that which is weed? I'm begging its trespass into
my yard, ply its errant length along my fence, try
tying it to me. Yet, long ago the stink of a polluted sea

found its own accommodation, long moved its lank
figure within our orbit, as smoke from my cigarette
crawled in wisps through our final barroom brawl.
Can I not be anything but maudlin. Snow's never
over. Nor are blossoms gone. Glasses forever itch in
cupboards to be filled with wine as mouths in dark
plot to be kissed. Recall how you once suggested I
sit by the sea to relax? I failed to admit the beach
here is littered with syringes. This is my good-bye.
I wish I lived in a little house by the sea. But I do.

WHY I AM AFRAID
OF TURNING THE PAGE

Spokes, spooks: your tinsel hair weaves the wheel
that streams through my dreams of battle. Another
apocalypse, and your weird blondness cycling in
and out of the march: down in a bunker, we hunker,
can hear the boots from miles off clop. We tend to
our flowers in the meantime. And in the meantime,
a daughter is born. She begins as a mere inch, lost
in the folds of a sheet; it's horror to lose her before
she's yet born. Night nurses embody the darkness.
Only your brain remains, floating in a jar that sits
in a lab far off, some place away, and terribly far.
Your skull no longer exists, its ash has been lifted
to wind from a mountain's top by brothers, friends.
I am no friend. According to them. Accordion, the
child pulls its witching wind between its opposite
handles: the lungs of the thing grieve, and that is
its noise. She writhes the floor in tantrum. When
you climbed the sides of the house spider-wise to
let yourself in, unlocked the front door, let me in
to climb up into your attic the last time I saw you
that infected cat rubbed its face against my hand.
Wanting to keep it. *No,* you said. We are friends.
I wear my green jacket with the furred hood. You
pushed me against chain-length. Today is the day

that the planet circles the night we began. A child
is born. Night nurses coagulate her glassed-in crib.
Your organs, distant, still float the darkness of jars.

DOGSBODY

It happened just after we did what we did.
Afterwards, paired cinders pinned their glows
on a dark aftermath, the room's black matte.
But who in this world will love the atheist?
It depends. Now I must get something off

my chest (which, for example, a certain pair
of god-fearing hands slowly finger-licked just
this week past). How can anyone pull one's
breath in at behest of God knowing he's a *he*?
Like Him, my love won't answer the phone.

Just like God, he's really got it going on. You'd
think it'd take me days to elaborate on his
particular beauty. To ask the moon for favors,
yet again, lend its light, well: it's excruciating.
I'm sick of nature's pawnshop. Yet, let's trade

in a few of his holy activities (my intent is not
to be sarcastic): digging small fossils up from
out remote riverbeds, standing lonely and sage
within the frame of sun-groped pastorals, and
twanging his voice at words the same way burrs

attach to a pant's leg, or catch at the fur of dogs
lost to the imperial immediacy of scent, and are

thus lost entirely to the voice that is the leash of
a god-lover, a dog-lover, for he loves a lost dog,
as any opposite god does. But it does no good

to imagine him when my god, my dog, is dying.
It does no good, I mean, because of the because.
My dog (happens to be) dying, my reverse God,
my good as dead dog, whose peculiar glistening
eyes are now lighting up on me sitting beneath

a window black with lack of light, the lit room
casting its appalling theater set back at the two
of us, for (thank the God that gave me my dog)
even my fearsome and fear-full love must admit
(will he yet confess?) he will not have me, atheist.

When it happened, it must have happened after
we did what we did. I made a mistake asking
him what he believed in. The lousy specter of
it: am I such a masochist that I come to fall in
with a Christian? (I always swore to myself I'd

never use the word *cunnilingus* in a poem, yes,
promised myself I'd never become so clinical,
so cynical). And I imagine he must raise a God
before him as one daily lifts a shirt, unfolds it
from out a dresser drawer. *What's-his-pants.*

Hey, what's-your-face! You dumb blue-eyed
trembler, your tragedy constantly undertaking
its making and unmaking, how comes it to be

that what you believe is incarnate? Is it Him?
Did He decide to allow you to allow yourself

to allow my mouth to let its throng stroke sleek
against your plumed throat? How can I find where
the why resides that says you won't ever again?
God? There's a dying man in my bed! How can
you expect anyone to forgive? My dog is dead.

HIGH SCHOOL: INDUSTRIAL ARTS

The lesson today is: someone always gets hurt.
Will it be you or another fool? This is a choice.
We provide the tools and materials. The saws,
the wood, nails, and supervision. Fall not now
in love, for it is merely a distraction from your
assignment. Now, create this uninspired name
plaque, build stacks of unstable shelves, lament
your lack of craft as the heat of your lust forms
in vaporous pools on the floor just below your
worktable. You thought this class would mean
an easy credit. Welcome to our workhouse. No
one leaves this building whole. Consider now
how this building's roof's akin to the lid of a jar,
tightly screwed, and you're the inhabitant within,
you're scrabbling at its glass, yet we've punched
no holes in that aforementioned lid. Now, make
something! Make something no one can use that
no one wants. Don't ask why. It builds character.
Someday you'll look back on these days fondly.
Here are your goggles. There's the eye-rinsing
station. No, this is not *art*! Ladies, stand back!
We don't want you cutting those pretty fingers
off or sawing yourselves in half. This is a man's
work. You, wipe that smirk off your face. Last
thing I need is one of you girls dying on my watch.

BLACK UMBRELLA

What to do stationed beneath an awning curtained
falling with rainwater but read books on dinosaurs?

Better to peel open tins of tuna for the stray cats
nestled wet beneath porches of the neighborhood.

No one wants them in their hunger, nor for piteous
cries to interfere with the sounds of the televisions.

If the town had one huge umbrella, we might all join
to carry it above us together. But there is no together.

Unless you can call a collection of structures *together*,
when all we've really got is a shambles of inhabitance.

Nothing throbs warmth near midnight, no clock can
admit its choking, and sheets have never had license

to speak. They hate us lying atop them, hate turning
in the washer, the dryer, over and over, as I am come

to despise someone I never saw in the rain. Someone
who has lain on my sheets. (I've not been discreet.)

One who rarely or never, you choose, gave me license
to speak. As the liquor store clerk demanded tonight,

Are you in a bad mood, or are you tired? I said I was
neither. He assumed that meant I meant I was both.

I assured him I was none. *See? Your expression, your
tone!* I told him he must be projecting, that I was sorry

he felt worn and alone. This is the price you pay in this
town when you neglect to hand your smile to no one.

But the cats would froth at your doorstep should you
attempt to feed them. You'd have to bat them back!

It's best to remain still in rainwater and read your best
dinosaur book, read it aloud loudly. For instance, you

might think they'll never come back. But I myself fear
I'm becoming one right now. That I'll roam this town

beneath a giant black umbrella I've fashioned for my
enormous frame. That I'll gnash my placid neighbors

in my jaws should they attempt to suggest once again
I ought to water my flowers more often. That's what

rain's for, friends! Just think of it as the sky's watering
can. I've bought the deed to this plot. I'm so American

I'll bury myself alive right here beneath this fatigued
rosebush, and my bone-mulch will push out petulant

blossoms pinker than ever. Because I stocked up. I got
supplies. The cats have my back. Because I'm trying to

explain myself while swilling water off my windowsill.
Ill-humored clouds from distant smokestacks please me.

Because that crisp smell you call *fall* I don't care about.

BAFFIN ISLAND

Some nights when the dusk is done hurting
the glass shards shaken out onto the street,

has finished stirring the empties' smashed
embers up with late light into fits of glint, I try

a little harder to remember. In the same
manner smoke alarms alert us to their

weariness by emitting a meagering succession
of beeps, you'll try my memory while I sit

back on my couch with a drink, feel for me what
it was to drop my eyes out a plane's porthole

into the maw I saw below: an ice-island lying flat
beneath, clouds layered between it and me,

an elderly lady in the seat beside me snoring
in Chinese, our craft shortcutting its way to

Hong Kong over the Arctic Circle. Understand,
I never expected my eyes to land on that land

on which your eyes flew from out your skull.
And that fortune teller I dismissed, who said she

could hear two boys knocking on our cloud
door, anxiously waiting to be born unto us.

Weeping into the cup of myself on the subway:
the kindest look handed down by a stranger!

A portrait in a porthole closes with one eye.
Remembering your hand suspending a jewel

of cheap wine shining garnet in a jelly glass.

EPISTLE, MANY-PRONGED

Mortification, I've known your corpse lips.
I've undone your pants, reached in to make
balloon animals. Once I twisted you a pink
and silver rabbit-eared hat. You squeaked,
I swore I'd someday Swinburne you. Later,
slumped over and listless on that bench in
the train station, I swore I could feel you as
you walked hurriedly past. Always know I
do not consider you obliged to return this
ugliness to my return address, this epistle

requiring a special envelope, one fashioned
to accommodate its many bristles, a sort of
crate that allowed it to continually stake its
blooms outward throughout postal transit,
a flight that allowed its origami hothouse of
hatreds to arrive, serve up its towering ups
on this simple, on this seemingly unspecified
afternoon upon your doorstep. It was never
a simple plant. Like most bad thoughts, first
it grew untended, loved being a weed-beast.

Like a nasty glance, it rose unbidden, as if it
had come into its own as soon as it was born.
Yet it had the sense to shrink when meticulous
neighbors began eyeing it by the gate in hopes

of trimming it back, so my lawn might appear
to have more order. I always suspected it had
a silence it worked itself toward, in the manner
seeds germinate in the dark, in the same way
a sack of potatoes will grow raw hairs inside
the cabinets that sit beneath our kitchen sinks.

Before long it buckled the sidewalk, suffering
me a week-long headache just in figuring out
how many stamps a ten-pound plant requires,
carefully wrapping it so it'd arrive undamaged.
Do its fronds now reach down into that joyously
peopled square you cordoned off inside yourself
back when I proffered the paw of my hand? You
yourself, being also *peopled with demons*, will
no doubt understand the lengths that I went to,
ensuring it remain intact throughout its transit.

THE HAMPTONS

Never shall I. The oily slow slide,
cars suctioned along firs roadside
luminous in rows. For what am I
hunting down stiles with stakes
of eyes, pulling up to Lilly Drive.
Don't tell me about the poverty
of the soul as people cross roads
ambling white with their turned
up collars toward caviar nights
now the sun pulls its hands off
those docks, unmolests sunners,
as folks in finely woven cotton
sleep in their walks from house
to car car to house. Never shall I
return for what's beautiful there,
nature slicked from out a wallet.
Moving along a near dead current
of cars, oiling my way toward my
host, a house I unwittingly enter
through the front door to be kept
out back, sequestered neck-deep
in a water hole, otherwise known
as a swimming pool, my daughter
clinging prune-puckered fingers
along my neck all afternoon, as if
this is a vacation: to be set out in
the plain blaze of all of that which

is terrible mundane, ah, it would
seem we ought to be grateful. O
how much of a giver the moon is
here, spectacular as the migraine
its sister sun's lent us, pastimes.
What here I am is plain poor.
Chalk my days, marks on a wall.
Cannot I like the moon, forgive it
for servicing the sky here too? Then
I thought too of you, the nature
disordered, cordoned, quartered
yet courted. I began to long for litter
thinking of your face, a face upon
which my eyes break seeing its ink
smear and crazy bloom, because in
the Hamptons, I'm a smudge, quiver
sipping iced tea for fear someone will
suddenly, industriously remove me,
bullet me off faux wood panel, sharp
squirt with the disinfectant jet come
from a spray bottle, wipe me clean off
from the where I was never meant to
be, that I long too hard on a wish to
park my tongue in the run-down garage
of your workshop mouth, give myself
back to what was once ours and now
I know to be a most exquisite poverty.
Never shall I allow love in again is a
notion I found myself at the end of
the end of the driveway that day I
arrived at to die at in the Hamptons.

MY FIRST HUSBAND WAS MY LAST

If not for this one fond thought.
Trees wave their violent weight.
Heaved in air with storm's hand.
They confiscated my hair elastic.
They confiscate my bra, as each
could twist into a noose, my bra
wire sawed into a shiv. And we
were both stubborn. Asleep side
by side until the night before we
would never again sleep side by
side, neither of us was willing to
be put out, sleep on the couch.
Falling into bed, he dropped his
mouth by my ear to mutter deep
You'll drink yourself to death.

Yet, we had much in common. We were both
nocturnal as bats. We both smoked furiously.
We each had a tendency to interrupt people

mid-sentence though we each hated nothing
more than being interrupted. We each had
a tendency to hurl death threats. Enormously

seductive on first impression, once our targets
succumbed to our wiles, we stared back at their
love, appalled, our eyes dead diamonds.

We voted Democrat and loathed the rich.
We considered our intelligence unassailable.
We were unbearable. Yet my fondest memory

is when he arrived to bail me
out of jail and I do not intend
a metaphor. He was the only
one who saw me wince when
they tightened the handcuffs.
It was for his ear I'd quoted
Keats while being walked in
to the precinct: *Forlorn! The
very word is like a bell.* Never
an early riser, he did not fail
to arrive at the jail near-dawn.
I saw him pacing before that
Plexiglased partition serving
as portal to the room in which
I stood wearing the obligatory
orange jumpsuit in an orange
blaze thick with the company
of other women who had also
done some bad things wrong.

(I'd run a yellow light—he wanted his late-night
snack at the Country Kitchen—heard a siren stop
us, thought in fright my bowels might run loose

down the insides of my pant's leg, trying to walk
true to the line, so scared shitless was I, I suppose
any man who ever hopes to know me must know
this about me, that that's why I drove that night.)

Yet it's also true that night foretold how a shadow can
    strive
to overshadow another shadow (some of us, apparently,
    wake
only for these sorts of battles), for though I lay silent,
    assigned
to rest on the cell's concrete floor on a thin pallet,
    thrummed
to sleep by my cell mate's snores, the thought that I'd
    arrived
at a punishment so terrible made me feel a certain kind of
    pride.
Like my dear friend who died (who was not my ex-husband;
    he
is, I'm told, still very much alive), told me how he threw
    him
self off from trees he'd climbed to see how he'd bleed
    when he
was a child, feeling the damp from concrete walls seep
    ache
into me became just another way I found to feel myself
    alive.

    Yesterday I received notice
    I'd failed to pay a civic fine,
    a "penalty" I incurred from

an arrest that the court long
ago "dismissed." Although
I distinctly recall filling out
a sum of 200 bucks for that
particular money order back
in 1999, payable to the Iowa
Dept. of Motor Vehicles, no
record of this payment exists,
though judging by the clerk's
sharp glee tickling the ether
as she read aloud my crime
from off a computer screen,
although fourteen years have
slipped beneath us all, and I
can't remember that town's
street names, I'll never buck
the mean notoriety of that sad
local newspaper's entry: DUI.

I was placed in a 48 Hour Lock-Down Program as
    reprieve, as a first
time offender admitting my offense, a program operat-
    ing, would you
believe, out the Heartland Hotel in Coralville: a bunch of
    drunks under
one roof being taught how to not use alcohol, reminded
    how each of us
had fucked up to the point each of us wept, among us a
    sixteen-year-old
who drove herself into a snowbank well over the legal
    limit, and me, I

was feverish to leave so as to be back with him, my first
    husband, who
had scored a good lead on pot from a friend I made over
    that weekend.

> Every bit of this is off-record. They confiscated
> my hair elastic. Even the mug shot, which I can
> only hope has been destroyed. Terrible-dark then,
> my hair rode its idiot storm atop my head. What's
> utterly queer yet remarkably clear in retrospect is
> how I felt a freak-urge to sneer or grin at the flash.
> They let me keep my underwear and socks. They
> confiscated my pocket change and wedding ring.

And if not for that one moment
when I stood within the gaggle
of orange-suited women (one of
whom growled, *Drunk driving?*
You'll be back!) that I saw him
pass before the Plexiglas as he
saw me, looked back, and he'd
mouthed to me against it all, *You*
look beautiful, my stare drained
within the fluorescence, could I
forget any of it ever happened?

> *He told me I would die* as I lay
> beneath our shared coverlet. He
> told a shared acquaintance I did
> not care enough for the written
> word. This was, in itself, blasphemy.

So I was the cunt who cut his vocal cords.
Or I was rich and hid my treasure.
He kept company with petty thieves.
His one friend stole coins out of laundry machines.
He's familiar to me as a dust mote.
He's familiar to me as the carved
wood masks we hung on our walls.
He's agape, always agape.

My first husband was my last.
He's my Love Canal.
It's a miracle anyone ever married me.
It's a miracle anyone ever married him.
He's digging himself up in Transylvania.
He's pulling the stake out of his heart with his yellow
    teeth.
His awful teeth aren't his fault.
He was raised inside a tin can.
He was suckled with corn syrup instead of breast milk.
I think of him at the polls.
I feel his thoughts collect like chalk dust in my nose.
I wake up in a sweat.
I wouldn't be surprised if I woke up next
to him tomorrow. We are celebrating
the Fourth of July. I have brought home
a rotisserie chicken, which we enjoy
pulling apart and licking its grease
from our fingers, and later we'll find
ourselves in our bed, the bed in which
we will make death threats to one another,

upon which we shall blame one another all
our bitter long-lives.

    I once slammed the door in his face so hard
    if he'd been standing an inch closer his fangs
    would've been knocked down his throat. Or,

    rather, landing ass-flat at his door's parting
    slap, tailbone cracked, I chose to clatter back
    down the hall, my pincers snapping through

    the smoke-waters we'd made of our habitat.
    The only reason we got married was because
    we didn't know one another. But it is not true

    that I chased him with a kitchen knife, ever.

POETRY MACHINES

I saw your new book today. Just after I saw your new
    book.
The day after I saw your last new book. It kind of looks
    like
all you do is write books. It kind of seems like a rose
    grows
out your mouth each day: on the bus, the subway. In your
bed, in the germs you spread when you forget to cover
    your
mouth while coughing. And it kind of seems like you've
    got
locked in your office some kind of automatic poetry
    machine.
Out your ears, daffodils and smokestacks. Or out your
    nose,
a poetry balloon grows. Out your eyes, an odd image is
    cast:
a wolf's head consuming an ice cream cone. It seems like
this is poetry. What am I coming to poetry for? A gnat
    sunk
in a bowl of milk? I did not know I wished to relive with
    you
that morning you sat across the kitchen table from your
    father
in 1978. He took his black. He will, in a later poem, have
    you

working on the car out back. A bolt falls from the under-
    belly
of the car to *plink* into a dish like *a tooth extracted*. This is a
metaphor. We need more cold sores, need more of what
    you
won't give us; give us some true ugliness. Your books
    arrive
annually, slick events appearing like the latest model of a
    car.
It would seem you do not consider the writing of poetry
    very
hard. Couple swan and cell phone. Pair two paralytic kids
    in
wheelchairs, hand the sharp light from hospital windows
    back
to them. Descend an imaginary ladder, climb link by link
    down
from out the window of your tiny apartment. March into
    your
local bookstore and demand to know why they aren't
    carrying
your latest volume. Shoot the cashier with your poetry
    gun.

HIGH SCHOOL AS REMEMBERED
BY THE DYING DOG

The dead girl and I are smoking pot by a rotting stream
    beneath
a suburban overpass when the lost dog approaches us. We
    make
up a silly name for him, we call him *Topsy.* We blow pot
    smoke
into his nostrils. We don't even bother to see if he's wear-
    ing an
identification tag. He is alone. He needs us. We cuddle
    him, he
runs away back into the wood, we call after him, *Topsy,*
    Topsy!
Our giggles flicker into the air like the light on and off
    the dark
water where we sit beside the mossy concrete, listen to
    thrums
of cars driving over us overhead. Somewhere in this
    afternoon
there is an endless spring, it stretches and stretches, until
    only
the dark sky tells us it's time to go home. We laugh like
    we're
drunk. We laugh a laugh that rolls a barrel of ink empty-
    ing itself

out onto the slow street. Now Topsy, a small white dog,
   is gone.
He's run away from us, he's scurried into the folds of the
   bushes.

DEAD DOG GOD-HEAD

In the mosquito-dark of this lurch-street, scary
kids' phone cameras flash to clasp their lights

on my sad drunk ass as me and my dog slowly
meander these streets in his endeavor to find

grassy patches worthy of his piss, for it's scents
most deeply interior within the sidewalk grasses

that gratify the love of my dog's nose, this living
dog moving so elegantly ahead of his own leash,

who's pressed his huge head gentle-hard against
my chest to tell his love. You who must have by

now evaporated, I seek you in this mineral dark,
you whose hand once pressed the softest yellow

fur on my dead dog's head, can you no longer see
me now move behind my new now-dog stalking

stinks with slowest assurance, wearing the skin
of a moon? So I seek you in my private violence,

in that terrible species of vodka bender you know,
and the sweat jacket I sleep nightly in wears spots

where cigarette butts have charred its sleeves with
holes. I wish you out from walls, beg you to appear

in forms vague as vapor, and leave messages a-slur
to anyone who might care at all, until all the lovers

are so sad my dog is dead they now offer up puppies
in an attempt to plug up the hole, except I no longer

own a phone to answer them. Dearest Membrane,
you died before my dead-dog died, were the last to

touch her buttery fur. But you're never now, you'll
never know me grown up, will not list with me old

together across a crosswalk behind my new old dog,
even though I beg mists to call you out. Take a look

at my dog, whose scabs and sores astounded even
me after he'd nearly been put to death by his only

known family. I saved him, he saves me. We search
for the loamiest of places upon which he may piss.

And it was like that for us once, wasn't it, finding
a private place to kiss? When it's become obvious

you aren't here anymore, and my head's dented in
with sadness, I must admit that I like to imagine it.

HIGH SCHOOL AS
THE PICTURE OF DORIAN GRAY

Can they feel, I wonder,
those silent white people we call the dead?

You are never not what you were, and queer
it is to see your own cruelty rise in a mirror.
It's not that masks themselves are lies, rather
our masks are us, therefore uniform: fear us.

In high school, my head droops off the stalk
of my wilting neck, lets its dolorous flower fall
to rest a cheek on the merciful cool of a school
room desk. I wake having no idea what century

I'm in, having dreamt myself Queen, a leaf, amid quailing
sounds released inside dungeons. It's Homeroom.
He walks in, refusing to recognize me, that's how
ugly I'm considered: the first boy I ever kissed

says he was too drunk to remember anything.
There is a factory that produces heads like his.
One day, I'll hear he's died from an overdose
and not feel bad. Like him, I won't feel anything.

It's long been my complaint: having a body. So
what if I could remake the brain that conducted
the lips that proffered to me my very first kiss?
Would it be a reenactment or a revisit? *Want*

to date rape? We'd roll to/fro across the floor
of that treehouse bombed on three different
kinds of liquor. Or, reframe our fix, make our
marriage prearranged, conduct an insistence

that each mouth return to the other mouth
for a second kiss? Not having to know waking
to my childhood bedroom, bubbling up, best
friend weeping envious in the bed beside me,

nor thinking *such strange windows!* Should I
now fashion that dead boy's head so it might
whisper back to me a compliment? But I was
just legs and nothing else. *You really should*

go outside sometime, instead of staying inside
reading books. You're pretty. You're pretty!
In that life, I'd become an alcoholic. In another
life, I'd be much happier as an office machine.

LET THE DAY PERISH

I was meaner than a flimsy dollar the change machine
   refuses.
I was duplicitous as a Canadian dime.
I slid through your town only to announce my prejudices.
And only to slip my tongue into the slot of your mouth.

Bade you come over. Covered your hand with mine.
Bade you lay down. Stroked your neck, allowed your
   story.
Bade you pull my body down. Bore me half to death.
This is where the what and when happens. Two

people on a couch, liquored up and lousy at the mouth.
I dislike everything in your refrigerator.
I criticize your cupboards, suggest you replace
your glassware. I pick up a broom when you're not

looking (yet you were looking) and sweep your whole
house out. I make a comment about your teeth.
(Mine are very fine and straight.) I complain about
the cotton/poly sheets. (They make me sweat.)

There was a light from your window that bore
right through me. I wanted nothing more than
to put my tongue to your teeth. I'd have licked
your whole house clean, bought you a crystal set

of glassware, laid down the dinner table with new
plates. I'd scrub your tub, your toilet. But perhaps
you did not understand my critique as servitude.
I was merely asking to be put into your employ.

I happen to like your mud-wash eyes. The mean
bags beneath your eyes. The jitter your hand does.
I don't actually care about anything but that.
Everything's been lousy since I left. Someone

smashed my car window just for the hell of it.
I am constantly harassed by thoughts of you.
I have made a poor investment in real estate.
When you took me out into your backyard

and showed me the koi pond you'd filled with
cement, it made me sad.
        Then you said you could bring it back.

DEAD FLEAS IN A DISH
READ AS TEA LEAVES IN A CUP

Purpling my nails, I pluck fleas from cats,
sit this way and that upon my lone couch,
feasting the future from August air. Fog
does not swerve, but shifts and pools its

settling into crevices, and in this way it is
like memory. Like memory is like the cats
scratching at themselves bad, till rust hues
and spots papers they've lain on, and I pain

at the last drops from the glass. Idiot aunts
foretell my future, those stupid twins aged,
zombied with their doctors' prescriptions:
one with dead spots in the brain (coupling

booze, Vicodin), the other cruising a methadone valley
somewhere along Sioux City, IA's flat: a delirious
recluse! My blood relations. Are not my chosen
love relations significant? What hatches such

growth, a grossly minute movement in carpet?
Humidity spawns the larval, announcing itself
with welts on ankles and, thus, this bulwark of
depression (I don't want to wake up), reminding

one of one's decisions, one's once-lover, till that
great dream finally arrives mid-morning, the one
one never had a right to, and in its eye I am liking
making my mistake all over again, and will not

admit it that, because love is love, and one must
hope beyond genetics: yet blond was my lover,
and blond is my daughter, this spawn mine alone:
eyes haunted by blue's hues, lit gray with hazard.

A flea touches down on her baby-belly, the spot
at which I press pressing on a diaper. She's crying.
House rife with vermin, you've been brewing me
up again in an old dream's cup, scalding my hands

with the steam lifting cruelly off a delicious tale
that's for years lain dormant. But back when walls
were dominant, must-eyed, moss-hued, for hours
unmoving my love sat before a trap he'd fashioned

for the feral cat a-hiss beneath my bathtub, still as
the glass of wine hung from his hand, tuna can
cracked, set before the cage's door he'd hooked ajar
with a taut length of twine. I love to think about that.

It makes me laugh when no one's around. It's years
since he tipped himself off a cliff, got smashed. Hands
crawl a body to scratch. A ruinous dream is back,
swashbuckling its path from back out my past.

MEMORY IN PLAIN ENGLISH

We were very drunk and not very merry.
Always, it seemed, the dismal end to our
evenings met us at the Staten Island Ferry.
Lady, they don't let you go back and forth
anymore, not all night, not ever. You want
to take the boat back? You'll have to get off

to get back on. It's a perverse rule invented
to prevent the homeless from sleeping too
deeply through winter nights on the heated
boat. Every evening find the City's pinching
its pennies. No, it's not merry: it is squalid,
the ferry, and it is drunk beyond all means,

as the crowd heaves to spill its gut-burst of
malt onto gummy floors within fluorescence
that appalls all. Let's face it, you're a tourist.
You're the kind who never leaves the boat,
except for if or when you let your eyes step
out momentarily onto land. You stare back

at windows; overhead lights allow reflection
only of the boat's interior and its inhabitants.
It's a mirror you were after. Now any beggar
would scoff, scorn your offering of fruit; it's

likely a product of a genetic transmutation.
Are those pears and apples you're handing me

organic? You could not have your romance in
this century, Lady. Someone would either step
on your foot, or puke on your shoe, and that
someone would not apologize. See that young
couple, their bodies blue with intricate tattoos,
trading their tongues in public? It's not just

true, Vincent, it's scary: I too once knew what
it was to move between islands through night's
tender. We loaded ourselves up onto that ship,
drunk as all get-out to get home and make out.
Bad endings aside, I still miss most of all those
night-rides, my love on the Staten Island Ferry.

AN ETIQUETTE FOR EYES

I don't know
if I wore glasses
when I met you

but I know
the last time
I saw you you

drank a drink
I bought you
with another

woman who
was far uglier
than I have

ever been. I have brown eyes, did I ever tell you?
Your eyes are too too blue, tell-all awful, and too
too pretty; you make all the girls swoon, and then
lament how harpies pound on your door, plucking
the very shingles off your roof, conducting through
their unanimous will a plot to kill your hive's queen,
fix a hose from the car's tailpipe to pump barnyard
dread straight into your ken, therefore you demand
I ought never wish to lie in your bed. I have black eyes,

did I tell you? But your eyes are damp blue, fingers in
winter blue, worrying about a prom date blue, never
washed a dish blue. Have I mentioned my eyes are
dead brown, dirt brown, stone brown, done with you
brown, screaming out in the streets I'm so drunk brown,
I'm just ignoring the noise rising up from streets asleep
brown? As in, as brown as dead leaves because my love's
eyes were dead brown and when he shouted down at
that drunk on the street that New Year's Eve from

my third floor window that drunk man called him
Whiskey Whore Boy. And his eyes were not wish-
wash blue, his eyes were mostly moss and trees,
not mojitos in a barroom, no, his eyes all gin-lit in
a hotel room on our last night were ice-cold, even
in his farewell he was bold, his eyes anyone might
have called plain, but they could at least cry. I am
sick to death of your blue eyes, fabric eyes, flower
eyes. I have brown eyes, plain and saying eyes behind

thick frames, glassy eyes handing themselves over
to you in buckets eyes, dig your hands into my black
soil eyes, my ugly eyes reaching into your eyes for
my twin eyes, look back at me eyes while your eyes
crawl the walls, cloud-blue, wandering off as milky
bosomed maids will look away from the eyes that
seek the crevices deep between their heavy breasts
that sway beneath the cows they bend to milk eyes.
Won't you have another drink from my silty yonder

eyes? I may look
plain but I've got
roses in my blood,

can bloom right
out the soil of these
here brackish eyes,

wander a limb across
the chest of your
country, unlock

the footlocker of your
desire with the tip
of my vine eyes.

ORACLE

Dead girls don't go the dying route to get known.
You'll find us anonymous still, splayed in Buicks,
carried swaying like calves, our dead hefts swung
from ankles, wrists, hooked by hands and handed
over to strangers slippery as blackout. Slammed
down, the mud on our dress is black as her dress,
worn out as a throw rug beneath feet that stomp
out the most intricate weave. It ought not sadden
us, but sober us. Sylvia Plath killed herself. She ate
her sin. Her eye got stuck on a diamond stickpin.
You take Blake over breakfast, only to be bucked
out your skull by a cat-call crossing a parking lot.
Consuming her while reviling her, conditioned to
hate her for her appetite alone: her problem was
she thought too much? Needling an emblem's ink
onto your wrist, the surest defense a rose to reason
against that bluest vein's insistent wish. Let's all
us today finger-sweep our cheekbones with two
blood-marks and ride that terrible train homeward
while looking back at our blackened eyes inside
tiny mirrors fixed inside our plastic compacts. We
could not have known where she began given how
we were, from the start, made to begin where she
ends. In this way, she's no way to make her amends.

A THOUSAND DEGREES

It's called a thousand degrees. Think about love.
Seemed what the clutch of potbellied women
in striped shirts were muttering drunk among
one another as I skulked past them on a 2 a.m.
street's sidewalk buckling with the heave of
July's late heat, skitterish and still drunk from
cheap wine I'd sucked down in the City before
boarding and then dropping off from the ferry
into my weary walk home and what they said

was true. A thousand degrees, not just boiled
down to the bones, or an ash, but mere steam
room of sentiment. Become a mist of yourself
so dense you can't see an inch ahead in order
to walk through the remains of yourself. That's
what it now seems these past years have been,
a daily consummation of a personal cremation.
(They never told me where they buried him.)
Think about love. It's called a thousand degrees.

And should those raw girls rob me (my purse:
its wallet, keys, phone, all my sticky lipsticks)
by calling the skulk of my shadow out, if their
belligerence shall waywardly crawl the street,
latch onto my figure (my crouching homeward
crawl) to manhandle the trinkets I heave with

me shoulder-ward in my fine leather purse, do
I attempt to explain myself? I don't want to be
such a witch as to grow a forefinger's coax into

a hook with which to draw my audience, nor
to live with a wart on my chin displaying its
single twitch of a hair. Yet, the corner bitches
who've never known gold may yet listen. How
it blinds to think of him. All that barnyard love
and hay's combustion, pure ignition. The body's
dogsled pulled through a terrible condemnation
of white, Arctic Circle of the heart: Baffin Island.
Girls, remember with me how casually he held

his cigarette between thumb and forefinger,
recall how he flicked the ash expertly into his
open palm, then rubbed the dead cinder off on
to his pant's leg. How he spat from the corner
of his mouth. All that white heat. Which is why,
soft-bellied ladies, I crawl by your howls along
these glass shards, shrinking from your youth.
Think about love. It's called a thousand degrees.
(They never told me where they buried him.)

CHILLY VOICE IN THE TROPICS

Be the voice of night and Florida in my ear.
Use dusky words and dusky images.
Darken your speech.

—WALLACE STEVENS

I.

Likely as not, or like as like, there was that moment
I could not dislike, somehow hinged sudden to your
side, I became your oar, slip, skiff, turned rudderless,
ran my hands fluid alongside your sides, skin so fine,

though had slipped through the bottle mouth of you
years before, then got poured out, and paddled that
puddle like a lame duck, imperious, yet injured none-
theless. A bottle of fancy gin smashed on a foreign

sidewalk, we slipped our shots back from the shards.
We love loving our memory. We are sitting knee to
knee. We are now hand in hand, and, why, we seem
to have laid our lengths side by side, cars parked too

close, we are rubbing the very paint off one another.
I am blue, you are blue, we blue hard into the dawn.

Once, I put the phone down, closed it on your mutter.
Once, I fell back against a wall, feeling your murder.

II.

Message me I should wait. So I must hesitate. Message
me *she's gone now can I call u?* It's always a blonde in
the corner. Her head's dropped its tinsel thread on your
navy jacket. It shines its totem. The saliva in my mouth

thickens to gag. You call when I'm in the shower. I call
when you're asleep. A mutual subterfuge. Why you, you
aren't even all that beautiful. Yet, your charisma pants in
how you speak, women undress themselves before your

talk's satin sheet. And I'm not the first to go under, to
    sink
underneath. So I wait. Alongside the blonde in the cor-
    ner,
can I not begin to hate her? She's so inconsequential, has
no idea she's being undone. You'd think she's dumb, but

she's merely being deceived, we both have lain on the
    same
sheets, proffered lips to the same mouth, willingly
    handed
ourselves over as if our soul-stuff was some dumb oyster
worthy of any mouth: an eroticism. We live for this
    fantasy.

III.

The problem the heart has is with going back and going
    back,
seeking its shell center, its original home. It wants only
    what
will make it feel un-alone. Abalone, our souls shine, and
    you
lie struck dumb in your cloud of worry, for you are sure
    death

will come. And it will come. Yet, we ladies line up out-
    side
your door, scour your kitchen, chill your beer, walk the
    dog,
as a respirator stocks up lungs with air. We care, us
    twins,
we triplets, no, we are more, we're a herd: our souls
    brinked

on a perch of want will shirk their shells before your
    dismal
eyes. If it weren't for your tongue, the candor of your
    slippage,
would we not move on? But we are, each and all, con-
    vinced
we are the one. And I know I am the one when we sink
    deep

into your cheap couch's cushions. It hurts our backs, so I
    rub
your back, singularly loving the silt of your eyes, corrup-
    tion
that is your lower teeth, it's American, and I've given in,
    my
heart bursting open strange blooms. I know I'm not the
    last.

THE APPARITION

To wish a ghost to press against your breasts.
To negate the wish that one wished to harm.
To intend the kind of crime that cannot be undone.
To dream the field of his barnyard-kind breath.

To withdraw one's intent to make a harm.
To desire an automobile that runs on breath.
To never it out of your mind your unkindnesses.
To further the dream of his hay-rough caress.

To be someone utterly good without a past.
To be one who moves without a sense of tense.
To get that ghost out from the walls for a kiss.
To pull his ghost out your head for a long talk.

To make it all up, unsay everything ever said.
To become so quiet you may as well be dead.
To unthink the thinking he did unto you: true.
To walk backwards across the campus lawn.

To move in rewind, reverse-time, across a lawn.
To let yourself pass his bright bent on the green.
To make it certain you were never once seen.
To step back from the fence at which your back bent.

To pull the very airplane down from that sky.
To swing him back up to where he stood once.
To put the mountain firm again beneath his feet.
What's it like up there, being a forever-person?

I've been hanging out on the corner of you for forever.
To remove yourself from the spot across which the huge
    shadow moved.
The barge moved so silently one could not have known
    just when to run.
No one sells soda pop, no one walks by whistling.

And who can run from the hand of a shadow?

DREAD BEACH

It's a kill myself kind of day,
the sun itself refusing to lend
its flattering light to the skin
that makes my face, its eyes
set as facets to gaze on a sea
churning its organs up upon
the shore lit beneath a hurt,

where the gassy water's salt
fattens and deposits its small
wealth of dead crabs clawless
among stunted mussel shells,
beach glass the worn lip from
Mad Dog, and someone's lost
his pants three times by three

wave-worn rocks, by the pyre
of piss-filled Gatorade bottles,
discarded tampon applicators,
two combs jagged with teeth.
I died here once. Before nothing
mattered. So I pocket sea glass.
In another life, it'd have cut my

thigh. But all that's here rusts.
A grocery cart estranged upon

rock. Mattress coils deranged
with fishing net, and the plastic
bunting that once plied hospital
beds is now a white zipper twist
round a pylon staking remnant

pavement to sand this worn-at
children's hospital a someone
said let the sea take away so as
not to have to cart its ugly onto
the inland. And when the dead
began to matter was when my
wrists began to stagger, beach-

comb sea glass. Dragging their
blood-nets all over. Back then,
I got my gift of fading into walls
simply by leaning. *First time I*
saw him, I knew I'd been done in.
See, your salt-crumpled pants
legs dead as sea crabs, thick tar

muddle glued beneath sun next
to a tire rind, that half-full bottle
of Visine lying on sand in wait as
if to proffer its saline kisses to my
driest eye: froth your terrible past!
O, but if you only knew. Back then,
I was so much better at being dead.

POEM FOR AN AWFUL GIRL

I'll hand her his heave-ho. I offer her an extra
arm, give her a golden drip of fat to ring itself
round the mantle of her hips, then I'll trigger
a slight tic that tugs insistent below her lowly
left eye, her moo-cow look, and if I've spared
her a spidering of veins along her thick thighs,
it's merely because I'm feeling kind. I return to

needle the canvas I've lately been stitching for
a pillow upon which I've decided his head will
eventually lie. I've been stitching her for a long
time outside this room as I've been imagining
her tossing her sneer off from behind, she who
considers herself the candelabra losing its fuse
to every darkening room she's leaving behind.

(And, yes, it's with a gasp that I consider how
she cannot know this yet, how this knowledge
shall someday soon unbecome her face as does
a most unwelcome announcement, such as that
regarding an imminent flood made to a town's
mayor, but I am getting ahead of myself here,
because there is in fact no reason she should

care, and this is likely the gist of it: I'm not even
a shadow in the corner of her room.) I am now

stitching in a room belonging to any other house
owned by any other landlord who owns any other
house she is presently residing in. I could sit here
all afternoon, scratch my crotch while plotting her
death, and no one would care; worse, not even her.

Were it not for such precarious boredoms, their
weighty responsibilities, the pastime of needlecraft
would not have been invented for women to push
their disenchantments through a painted canvas
with thickest needle. Late into the night, stitching
deep. *If I had an extra arm, I'd move faster on this
project,* I lament. *My pillow shall a flower depict.*

YELLOW RUBBER GLOVES

Sisters, why bother? The telling is done.
I once fancied myself centaur, sweeping
floors with my tail as my arms sunk deep
into dishwater, half lost, indeed, looking
almost as if they'd been clean lopped off.
Mopping up all that blood, rusty strings

on the mop dragging their fat hairs along
the linoleum: I'm never surprised when
someone calls me lady. They may as well
call me a cleaning lady. Though I know
they mean *Lady!* As in, *What the hell do
you think you're doing, Lady?* I am merely

washing dishes. Yours. It makes me want
to give in, adopt those dozen cats, makes
me nervous enough to count how many
cigarettes I've got left. I've seen the lines
inching across my face. I'm wise enough
to know no great plans are afoot, I've no

hope of launching any ships, and, besides,
I'm done with beauty. They say the hands
go first, then the eyes. Then you get a little
pinched, whiskery around the lips. I'm not

adverse to invisibility. I'm already used to
getting shoved aside anyway, sitting small

as a pin between men spreading their legs
on packed subways. I'm the blunt cunt who
should have known long ago it's about time
I shut my fucking hole. But bring my hands
deep into suds, watch me muck with the dirt
of men's dishes, you'll see I really know what

I'm doing. My advice: yellow rubber gloves
will save your hands, young bitches, awful
twats who think you'll never be me. Trust
me as I never trusted myself. We're in this
together. Look at your hands! Who else did
you think he had in mind, undermining your

time by leaving dish after dirty dish behind?
And try using a milder solution. It may bubble
up less, but, being less caustic, the fewer skin
cells it destroys. Who do you sleep beside? Also,
lotion is important. Apply it just after washing
dishes and every night before you go to bed.

PLASTIC COOKIE

Like a teapot, I'm tipped to spill from my kettle snout
some silver tears, these few drops that glow and drip

their arrows down into the ground from off my eyes
and nose. I was going to send back the plastic cookie

fallen from your daughter's false stove, her pretend
kitchenette, into the net compartment that opens up

beneath my daughter's stroller when its pink flower
is broken open, which I discovered upon landing in

Newark, to push my nervy daughter along bright
airport corridors so that we might be reunited with

our luggage. My orange suitcase pops its atrocity out
from that mystery mouth that spills onto the metallic

fins that spool around, and I run to clutch at it, heave
its weight. Yet, just yesterday, it sat fat in your room,

contents sprung: underwear, diapers. The both of us
fearful for our respective daughters, too deep, perhaps,

in love with our singular daughters, drinking late into
the night, speaking of our daughters. Earlier, furious

your fearsome daughter pulled her entire plastic kitchen
down, crashed it to the floor, as if toppling a bookshelf

with the simple tug of a hand. Daughters astonishing
daughters! Mine with her dish-wash hair, plate eyes

full of gray-blues, wanting to play with your daughter's
stove, the plastic kettles, teacups. Still little, wobbling

all over the room. Then dusk sat its fat ass down at last.
To our great relief, we found our daughters deep asleep,

and were free to drink the rum of us, which was, as it
always had been, a gradual drink. And you know what

you know with your hands, wish the night blacker since
blackest is forever. Who'd believe I'd be dropping such

bells of tears now, to hear them ring inside the earth that
absorbs them? Let us not hand down this history to our

daughters. Let's ignore what a *plastic* cookie means to us,
or for that matter why your daughter had one in the first

place. Forget your daughter's pale glare in that doorway's
3 a.m.: innocent us lying underneath and atop one
    another

on your lousy futon. *Denier, liar, totem.* You'd given me
a plastic cookie. *No.* You and your daughter gave me and

my daughter a plastic cookie. You cannot now comfort
me.
So disown me. The soil is free. Within it lives all that
matters.

One day, I'll see you down there. Daughter-free.

DEAD GIRL GANG BANG

Though I can't recall your last name
now, Howie, I've been penciling myself in
to your way back then, way back
when, in your gangbangland, she was
loose and gone, struggling up on a limb
to raise herself off from your bed, but lost,
fell back, let the all of you in again. Said
just trying to get out your room

was no use since she'd got her own
self in. Curbside-mind, I venture
you are still alive. Wondering what she'd
think of that, but, then, I don't
know, can a ghost think when its body's shot
itself in the head? Hell, just thinking about
it makes me wish I were dead. Just
some girl, you, then you letting your friends

shovel their coal-selves up into her, just some
person. I knew. Her mother's now offering
a twenty-percent discount for crystal
healing therapy on her website. In high school,
she was a calm mother, dull job as telephone
operator, back in that town her dead
daughter and I always swore we
would leave, back in that town dead to me,

and me, I marry a man who mocks
me for crying. *We-we-we,* he calls out,
snickering in the gloom. Yet still I wear the dead
girl's perfume. And I've got an accident
to report. Because it was all our centers,
uninvited, you rucked up inside, then bade your
friends park their reeking selves in the garage
of her feminine. What did you call it

back then? You balding fuck, you've forgot.
Sloppy seconds. Forgot her slippage, eyes dead
drunk spirals, face some fluid spilling down
your sheets. I've been where she's been,
and I can be where you are now, switch my hips,
sashay into your office to see you any day now,
wearing her perfume. What pack animal
would you choose to be in your next life?

Every day, the marsupial clouds grow
hungrier for our reunion, the reunion I've been
packing for all my life. There is a swing set
and a girl in a dress who doesn't know about this
next. First, she's pretty. Finally, she's done for.
So I took some pills to forget I knew you last
as friend. Then I learned the ways of your wiles,
how you did my girl who's now dead in.

AFTER AFTERMATH

Orphaned boys plus my mean calculations.
Orphan boys plus desire equals their long
bodies. How they sucked summer-long water
off a garden hose from beside the trailers.
Their mean mothers weary of them sharing
rooms in mental hospitals: I want to meet
them with flowers, thank them for offering
up their sons to this, our glazed Plexiglas
world. What would we do if not for them.

If not for them, *how could I breathe.* How
would I know what to do, if I did not have
to care for them because they learned how
to not care for themselves because of you.
Orphan boys make mean men. Because of
them, I feel mean. I make my calculations.
Because I love them, am loving how they're
dropping off the other end of their phones.
They hang up on me. You hung up on them.

I am tired of your ultimatums, Skunk Mom.
My eyes squeeze. I'm unhappy with you, Mom.
You're not my mom, but I'm calling you Mom
now that I'm his mom, Mom. Your son can't
say what he thinks because you didn't teach

him how to articulate himself, Mom. *Shhhh,*
your beautiful baby's asleep. I'm a mom too.
You left him alone in that room that night he
heard you rucking on the sofa, Mom. Said he

saw a ghost. It shooed him from the doorway
so he would not see you fussed up on a sofa.
He was just a little kid, Mom. But I get it. Kids
forget. I've got your kid in my bed now, Mom.
It's inky in here, where you forget him, Mom.
I love him as stars lick our faces with the nose
wet cold of cat kisses. I had thought of men
as flowers. I picked a few. Then I met your son,
Mom. He's still weeping flowers to that belt's

swish in your basement. And isn't it on nights
like this, Mother, the thought of killing yourself
looks you head-on, beautiful in the face, velvety
and faithful in its gaze as that of the violet iris?
This is men, Mom. Your mistake was begetting
one. Mine was letting him in. He's asleep now.
Shhhh, your son is safe. What about you, Mom?
What about me? We're only daughters. Who's
become our father? Your son, Mom, your son.

HIGH SCHOOL IN SUZHOU

They play ping-pong. They are all boys. They play
ping-pong ceaselessly in the vast gymnasium, will
not stop to glance at us visitors from the West, will
not untie their eyes from the tiny ball. The principal

of the school, salamandered-slick hair, is displeased
the visiting professors are female, leads us out from
the gymnasium with silent loathing to a mentholated
room inside which a hazed Plexiglas cage contains

a stiff leopard, so frankly dead its fur looks as if it'll
fall off from the stroke of our glance. I have to pee.
In the Girls' Room, I squat where thousands of girls
have squatted, the rich minerals wafting up from

the toilet's well, imagine how all of our urine moves
through the mysterious pipes below, leaves the high
school, depositing itself into the river that days later
I'll move along with the throng of idiots I've joined

to crawl this country as fleas do a dog. We visit one
scholar's garden after another: here's the Garden of
the Master of Nets. The rocks are *bones of the earth*.
The furniture is referred to as *internal organs*. Gardens

are *traditionally entered through a narrow passage.*
Scholars were not girls. Girls are not scholars, though
girls are gardens entered through a narrow passage.
The girls at the textile factory we tour do not look up.

The guide snorts. We have no conception how lucky
they are to have attained these jobs! It's only natural
they wear masks to protect their lungs. In high school,
I was the Master of Endless Failures, thrashed nightly

in bed, on the verge of coughing my lungs out, in that
Garden of Spitting Up. And didn't every girl have her
garden? The Garden of Jutting Neck-Bones. Gardens
Pocked with Black Eyes. The Garden of Letting Him

In Despite Many Protests. A dead leopard relentlessly
sheds its fur above an auditorium of children hurtling
toward adulthood. In that gymnasium, there were no
girls playing ping-pong. They are all boys, ceaselessly.

SLAUGHTER AND WISTERIA

I don't like to be tickled, and I don't wear panties.
It's *underwear* I wear, and I've got space issues.
I really liked the Mom-'n'-Pop version of neighbors
I bought along with my neighborhood, the way
I imagine people enjoy venison in western states,
and I liked their house being tidy up-close to mine,

tucked so close I feel the wife tickling her piano's
keys without having to press my ear to my wall
so as to hear these neighbors who've resided in
this neighborhood as many years as it takes to
raise two children now married both: doctor,
banker. But I don't like taking my neighbor to

the hospital after he's suckered me into driving
him to the shopping mall just so he can buy a cell
phone his wife thinks he can't afford, all while she
is out of the country visiting her dying mother.
But I think I handled the situation well when
that car struck my car, and my neighbor, sixty-four

years old with a slipped disk, felt my vehicle shift
upon the impact, complained of back pain while
we waited for police to arrive after dialing 911
and the firemen arrived to strap him flat to one

of those boards, and we then covered him so as to
protect him from the evening's chill with a bunch

of tossed-off baby clothes I dug up from my car's
trunk as he lay prone, all us crowded waiting for
an ambulance to relieve us by rescuing him. Then,
I waited at the hospital for his discharge, sat by his
gurney, watching with him helplessly as ER admitted
drug addicts twisted against the leather harnesses

that strapped them back to hospital beds, and then
afterward drove him back to his house sitting up
snug beside mine. I'll admit, I always enjoyed his
laugh, but, truth is, I admire most my neighbor's
twisty wearied wisteria tree struck up sun-wise
before their front door, its head-full of hair wildly

purpling the street's atmosphere. I wish that he'd
not reinvented my face as *flushed* that night, regret
he penned those repulsive missives enumerating his
desires at dawn. It's why I no longer talk to them.
Not him, nor his wife (who recovered so remarkably
from breast cancer the year before), with whom, he

claimed, he no longer has much in common, despite
the fact their children are closer to my age than theirs.
This is why I've been hiding behind my door, why I've
not spoken to them all summer. And if you think I'm
unhappy, you're onto something. Today they chopped
that wisteria's purplings down to a stump. It seems,

surely, a message, at the very least an act of massacre.
My veins take on a stupor. I can hear my neighbor just
outside my window, speaking to a passerby. He's smiling
and leaning warm onto his cane, gesturing at a pile
of cleanly chopped sticks. If you think I should talk to
him, you're wrong. I have other things to be sad about.

But now he's got my attention.

ELEGY FOR A FAMOUS AUTHOR
NOW ASLEEP IN BROOKLYN

You're a walking elegy for yourself. Yeah,
you're one inch worse than being in love
with the dead. You don't know the dead
are perfected. They teach us what we had

wished we'd learned when they were not
dead. You, crazed in fear of death, refuse
to know that conversations with the dead
are divine. Being dead, they are not forced

to console or confide. They'll never report
It's been a bad year to any stranger they've
just met at a cocktail party. They are one-
way walkie-talkies echoing our love back

at us. They are satisfied shaking our dreams
out like tinfoil, smashing vases as we naïvely
enter into doomed telephone conversations
with those they wish us not to love because

the dead know better than us who's worthy
of our love and this is because they love us.
Their breath fogs up our mirrors, their deer
appear nose-close at dawn, slip their white

tails right out from sight, the dead are less
than obvious. It may be they like to give us
a bit of a fright. God knows they cannot help
but remember. In this way, they are like us,

for they are alive. Unlike you, who introduce
your eulogy at every plastic event, they've no
tombstones on their brows! And I'm up to my
bones with tragedy, yours being at the top of

my list. If you listened, the dead would suggest
you take a pill. Don't you know they want back
into this life, that they want to vote in the next
election? It's no wonder I could never love you

better than a ghost. You're a trembling mess!
Unlike you, it's the dead who've been dimming
the lights, sewing their sequins onto my dreams.
It's the real dead who know how to love me back.

NEXT OF KIN

The pastry shop's caught on fire. Baby waves
at the fire truck. Like any baby, Baby waves at
anything and anybody. That bus that drove us
immediately past the flames ate up the pastry
shop. Baby's confection unto herself, which is
why Mother hands down that look saying you
have no right to even *think* of slapping Baby.

Baby's small and smug as a snail, neater than
a crisply tied bow, wakes daily cleaner unto
herself soiled than we do walking down aisles
formally garbed, gifting ourselves unto death.
That she-bastard baby, always waving! Nerve.
Mother's moving through rooms as if nothing
strange's occurred, as if the baby's come from

nowhere but her own body, that baby waving
at everything and everybody. Nerve. Whoever
heard anything so sad as what that baby will
have to go through? She refused to disclose its
paternity. Is it a lap child? (*Mother is boarding
a plane with Baby in tow.*) And how come that
baby's hair's gold, when hers is dark? Strange

eyes, it's got, oh, not to mention all those rows
on rows of teeth: how does she manage to feed

it? (*Excited, Baby sank her teeth into her mother's shoulder.*) Now everything's burnt down, and all that baby does is smile. Dogs snarl like insults hurled in our kitchens as Baby drops morsels off her high chair's side for her dog to snap up

snappishly. *Good girl,* murmuring, she touches electrical outlets outright, shakes her head *No.* She's been told. But who cares where a baby's come from once Baby's arrived? All the sugary shops are done for. Baby's hair grows like floss straight off her skull. She is candy, she is cupid, she is grunting and pooping. Mother with dun

hair and smudged eyes yawns as Baby waves at an ossified hotel, at the worn lovers in check- out lines, at the mad old woman with mirrored sunglasses perched on the noble deck of her face, because this much is clear: Baby's got years on you. She's welcoming this bad world, she'll grab your sad ass and spit you up on her pinkest bib.